PLAY GUITAR W   2

(1980-1983)

PLAY GUITAR WITH U2
(1980-1983)

Wise Publications
part of The Music Sales Group
London/New York/Paris/Sydney/Copenhagen/Berlin/Madrid/Tokyo

Published by
Wise Publications
8/9 Frith Street, London W1D 3JB, England

Exclusive Distributors:
Music Sales Limited
Distribution Centre, Newmarket Road, Bury St Edmunds, Suffolk IP33 3YB
Music Sales Pty Limited
120 Rothschild Avenue, Rosebery, NSW 2018, Australia

Order No. AM955922
ISBN 0-7119-8216-3
This book © Copyright 2004 by Wise Publications

Compiled by Nick Crispin
Music arranged by Arthur Dick
Music processed by Paul Ewers Music Design
Project Editor: Tom Fleming
Printed in the United Kingdom

CD recorded, mixed and mastered by Jonas Persson
All guitars by Arthur Dick
Bass by Paul Townsend
Drums by Brett Morgan

www.musicsales.com

Out Of Control

Words & Music by U2

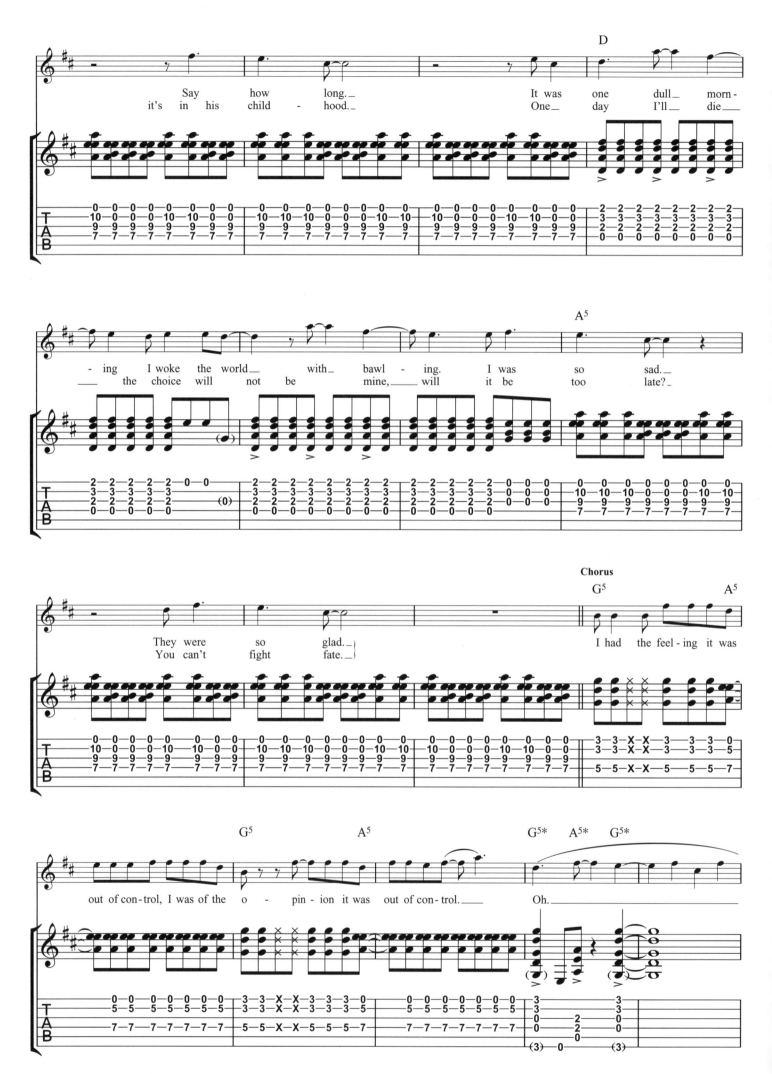

8

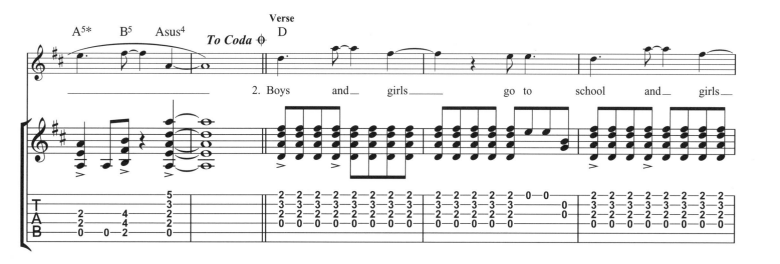

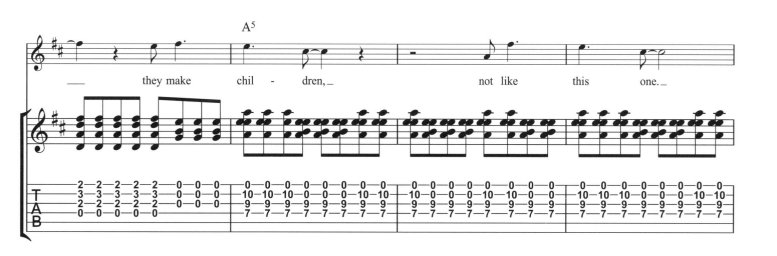

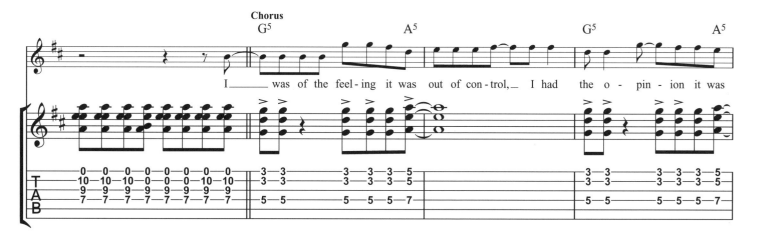

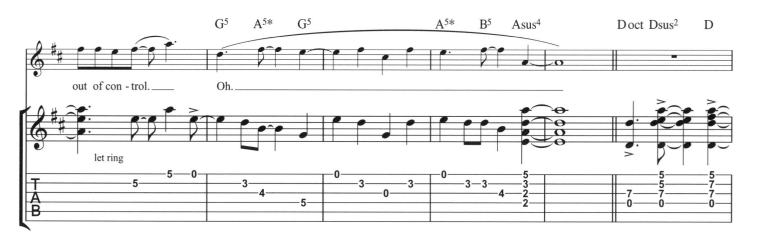

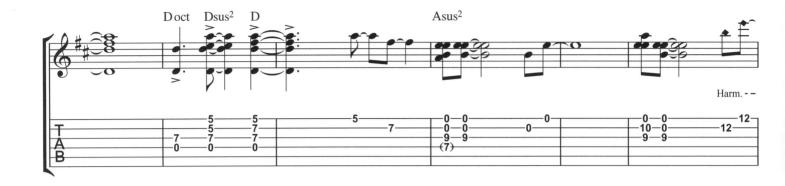

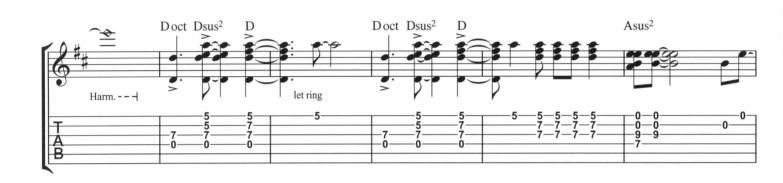

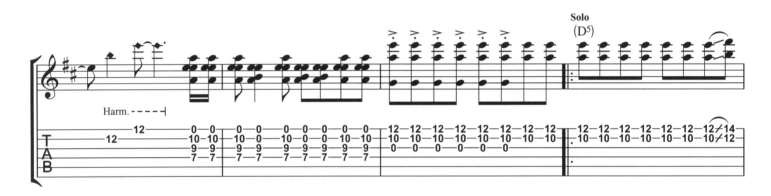

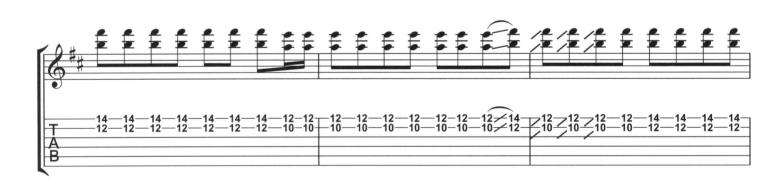

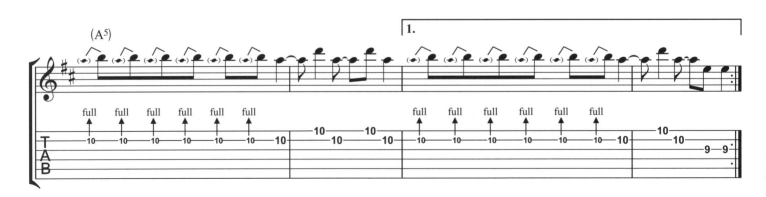

I Will Follow

Words & Music by U2

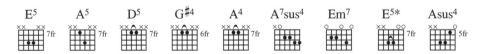

Tune guitars down a semitone

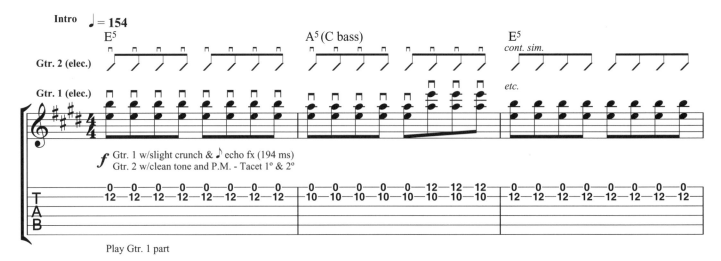

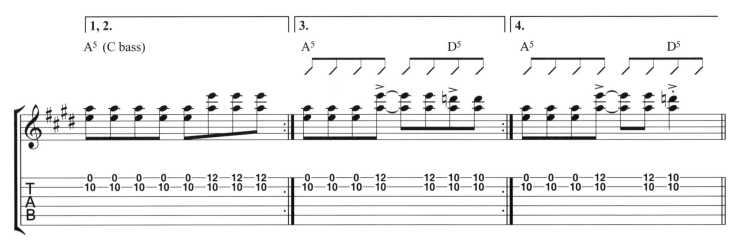

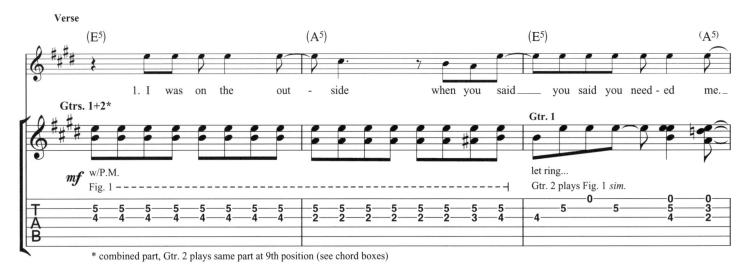

* combined part, Gtr. 2 plays same part at 9th position (see chord boxes)

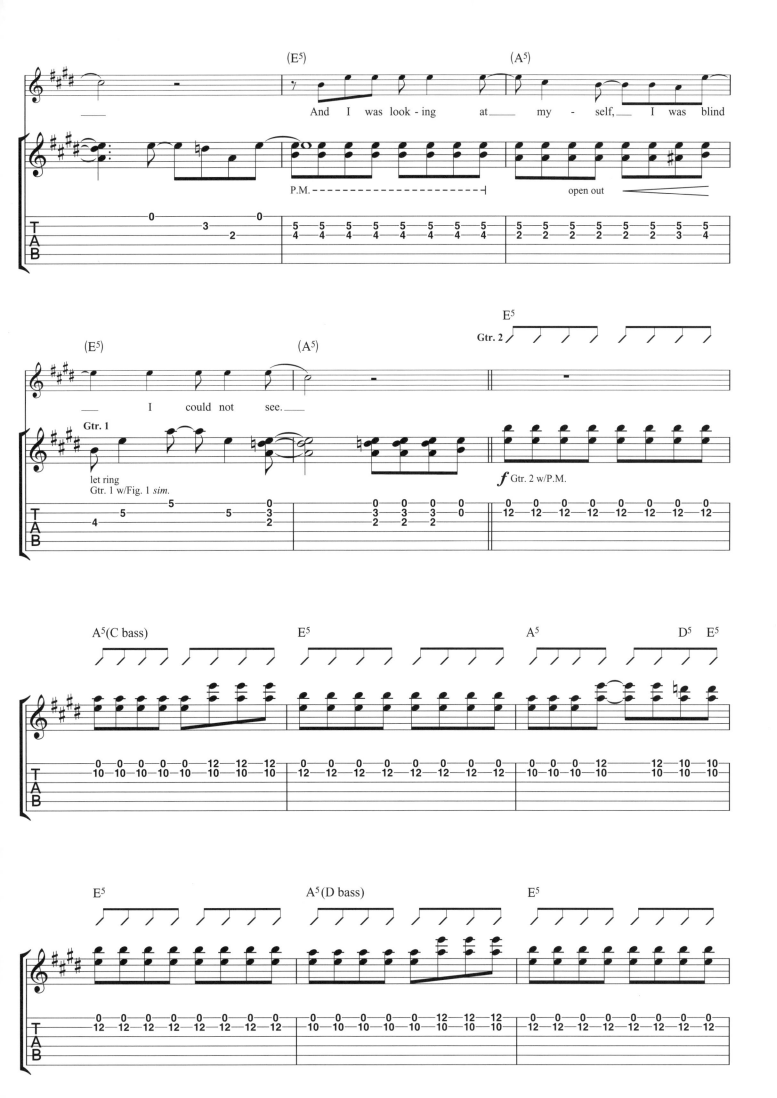

* combined part, Gtr. 2 plays sim. at 9th position

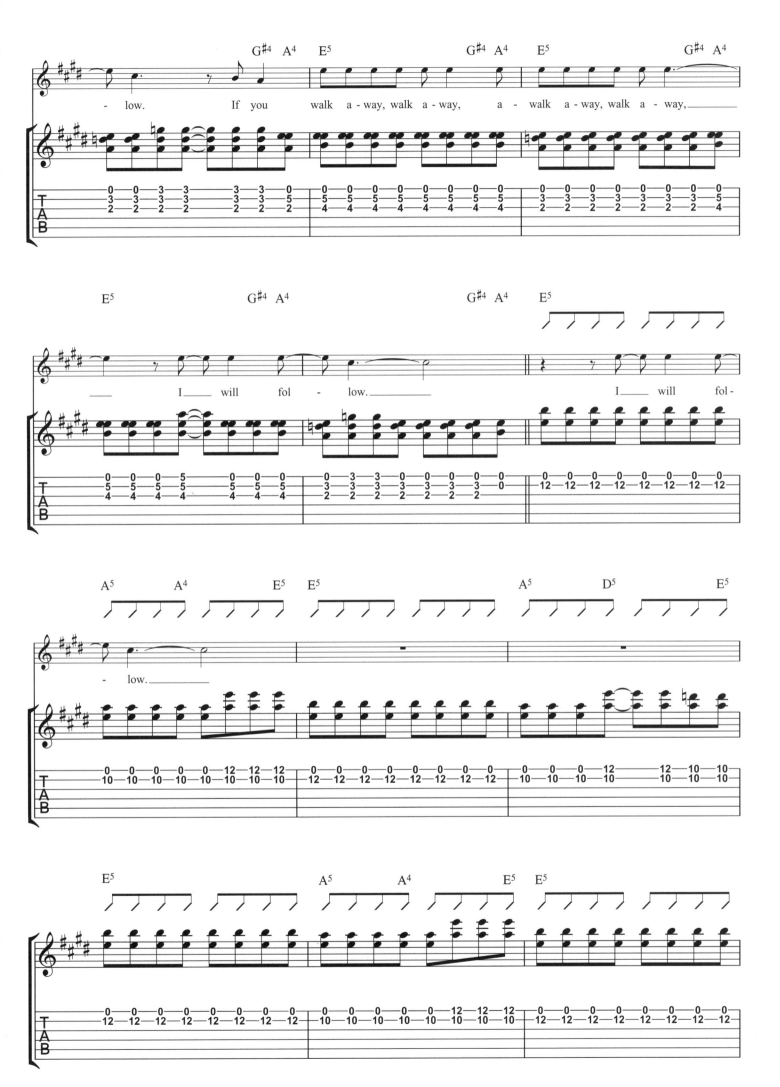

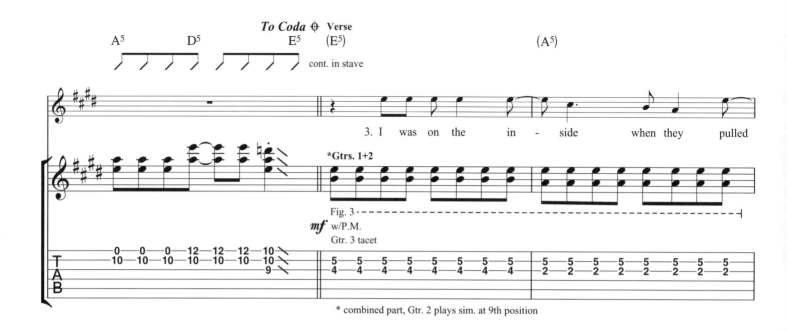

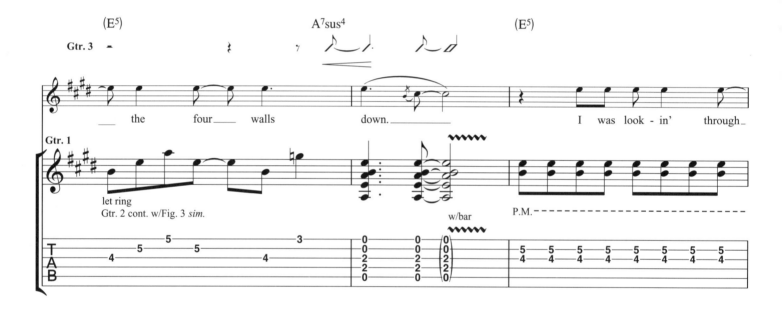

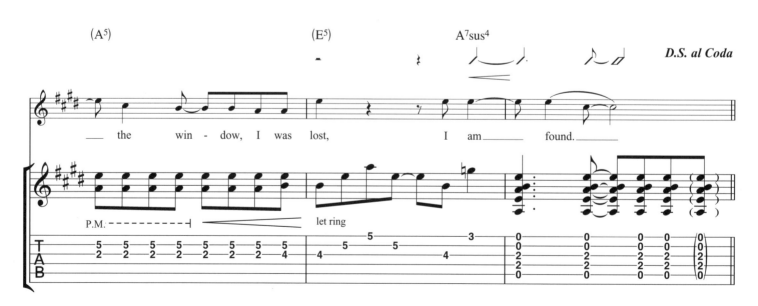

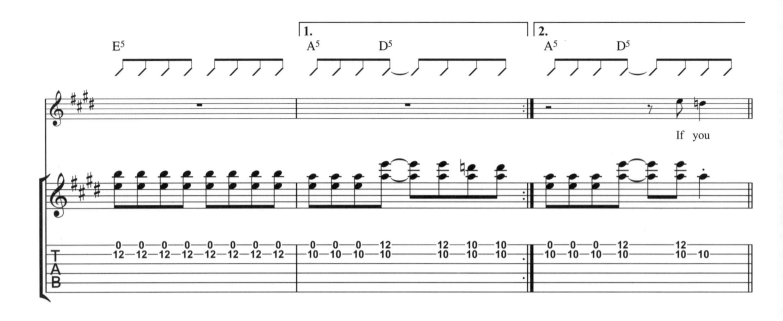

Chorus

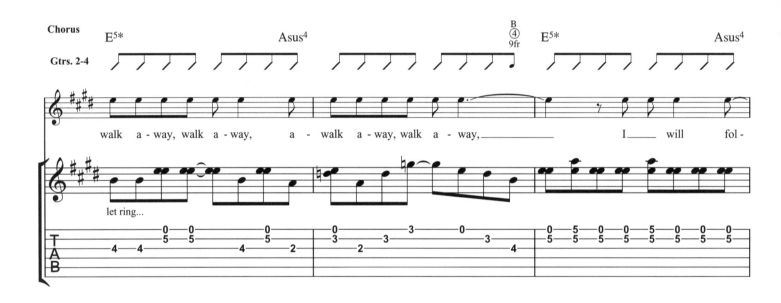

walk a - way, walk a - way,   a - walk a - way, walk a - way,_____   I____ will fol-

- low.   If you   walk a - way, walk a - way,   a - walk a - way, walk a - way,_____

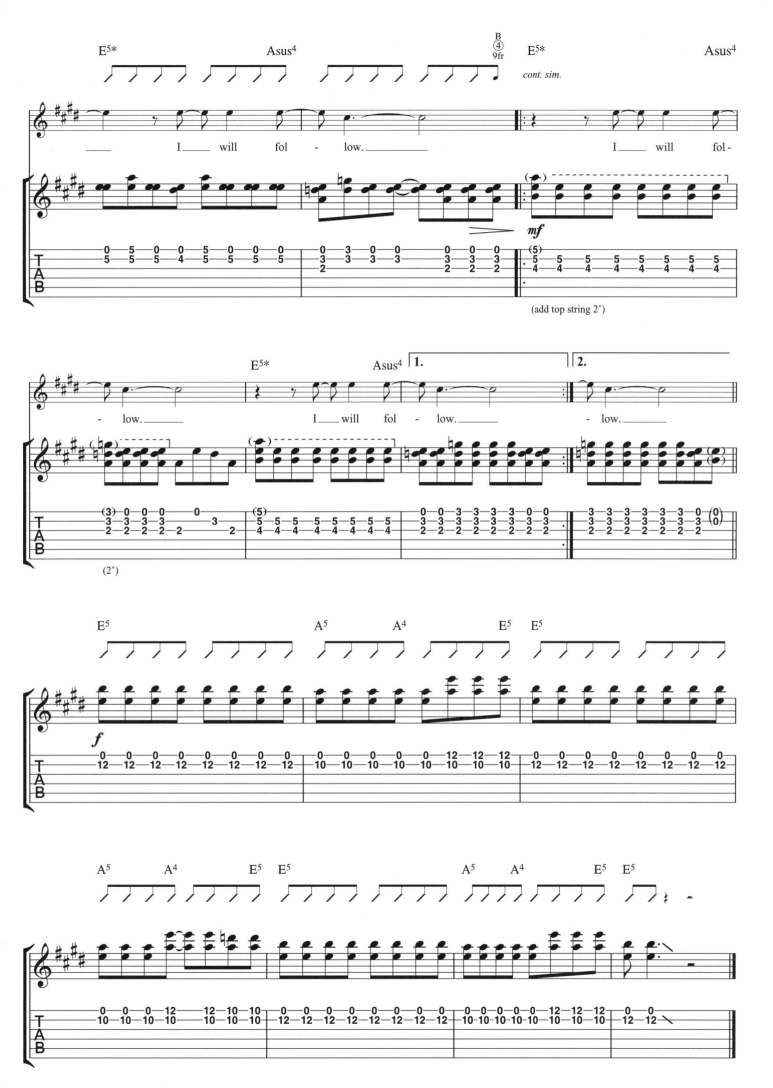

The Electric Co.

Words & Music by U2

Tune all guitars down a semitone

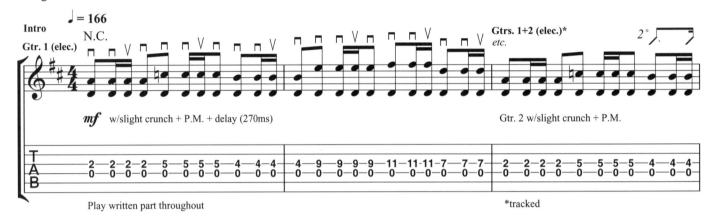

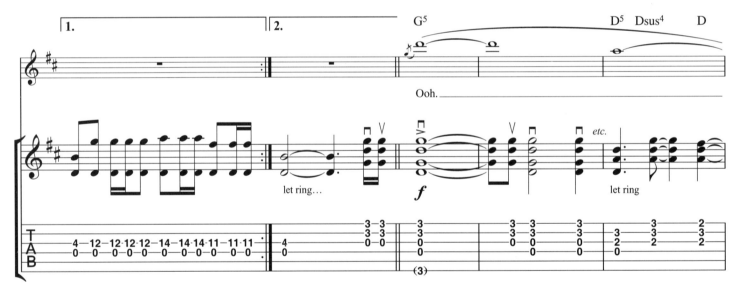

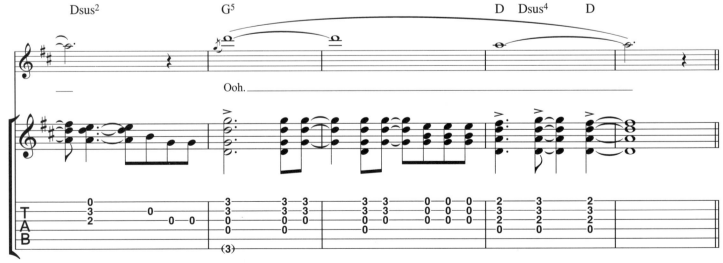

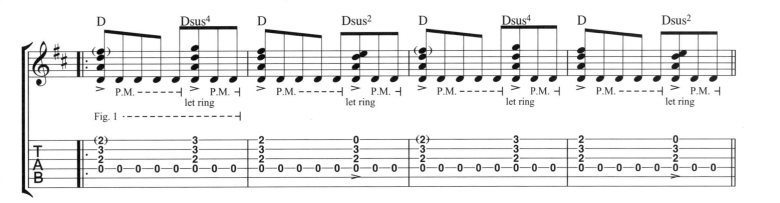

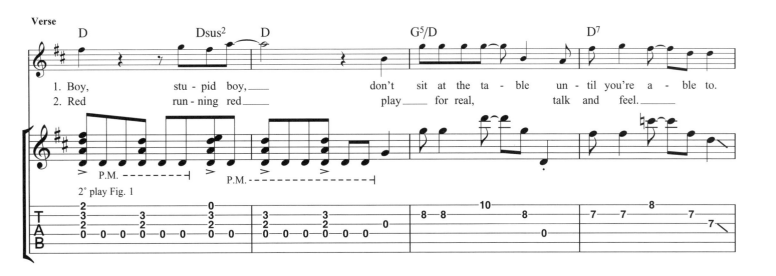

21

Gloria

Words & Music by U2

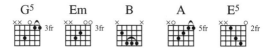

Tune all guitars down a semitone

give it to you.   I _____   give it to you.

31

Sunday Bloody Sunday

Words & Music by U2

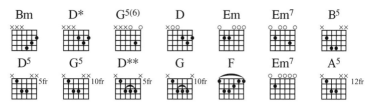

Tune guitars down a semitone

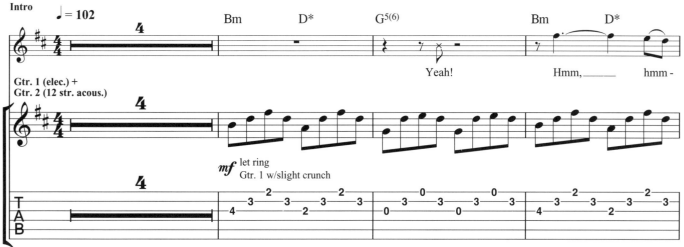

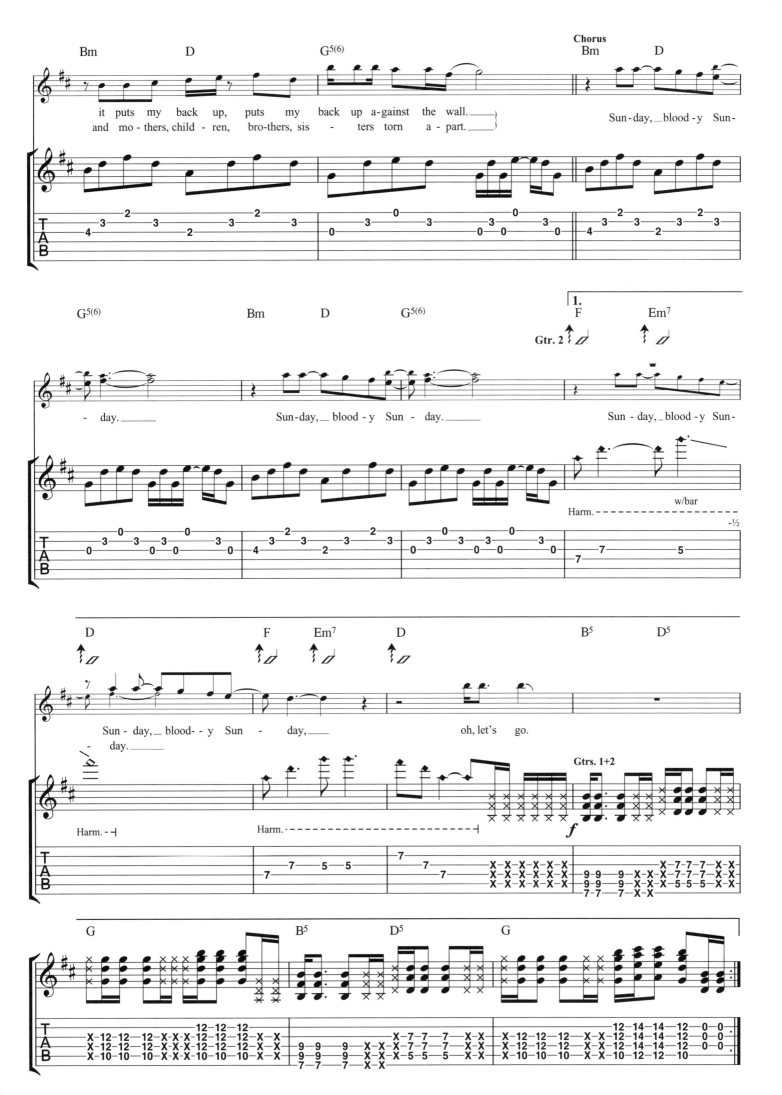

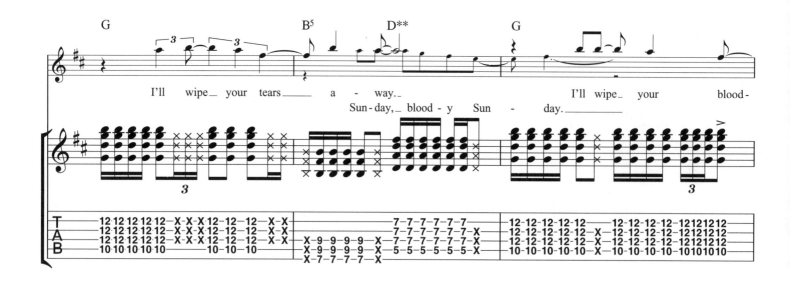

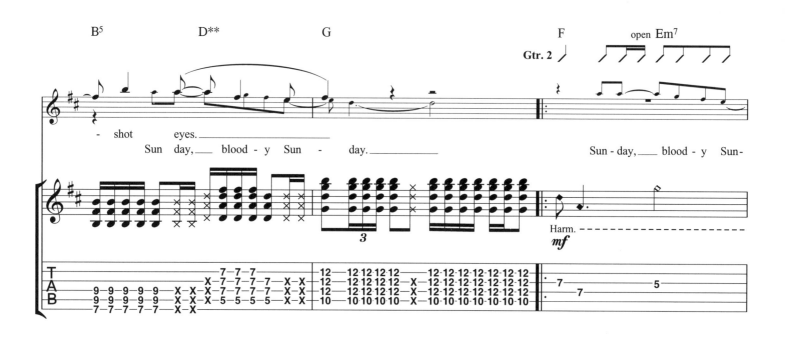

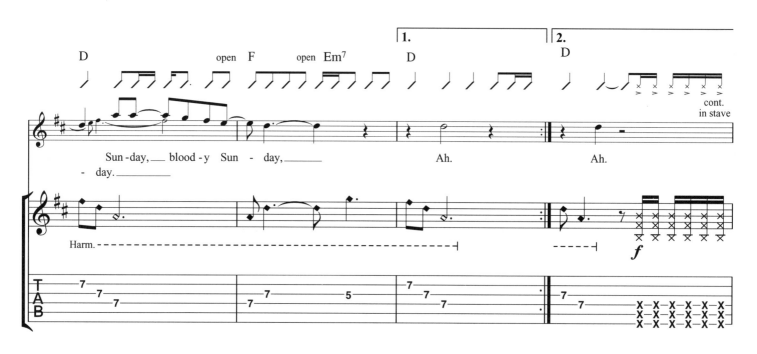

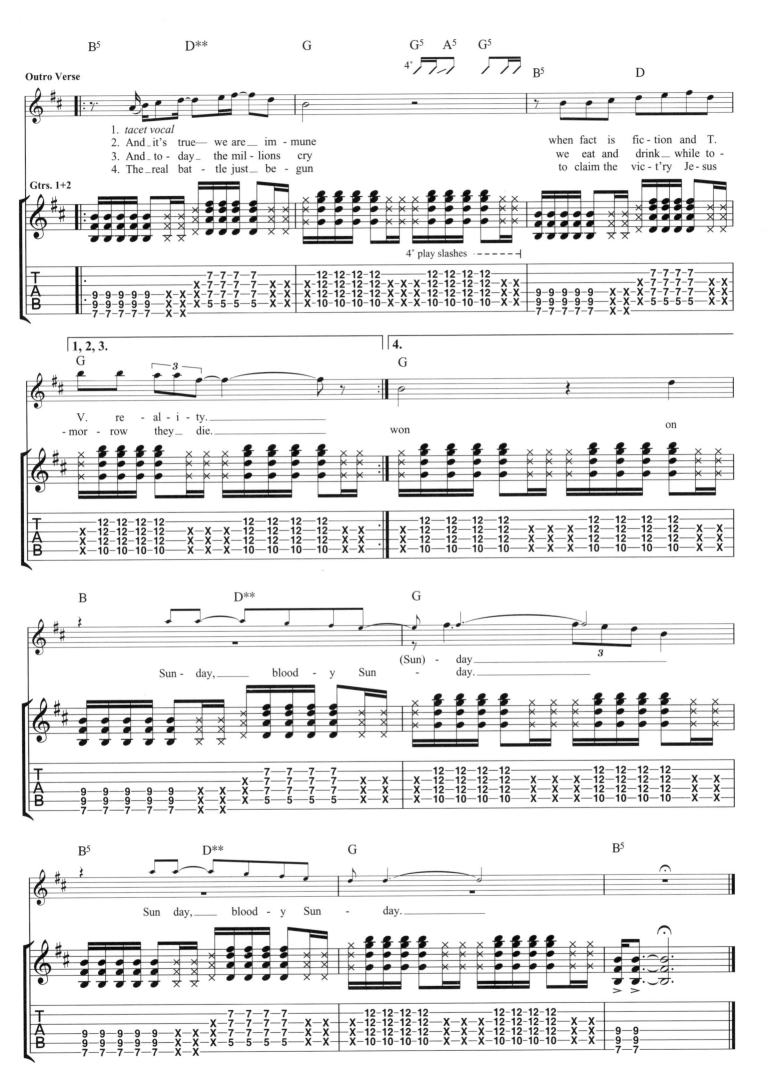

New Year's Day

Words & Music by U2

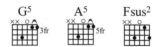

Tune all guitars down a semitone

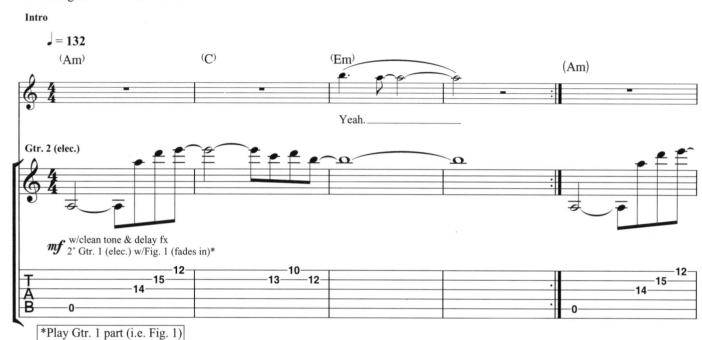

*Play Gtr. 1 part (i.e. Fig. 1)

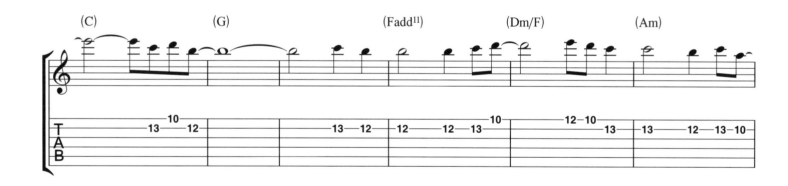

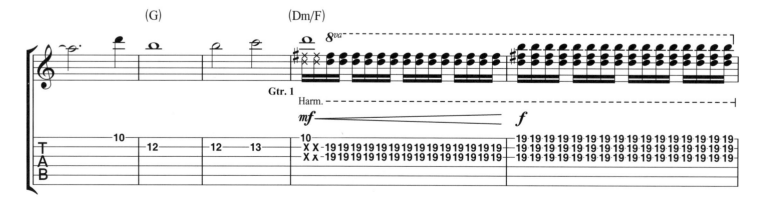

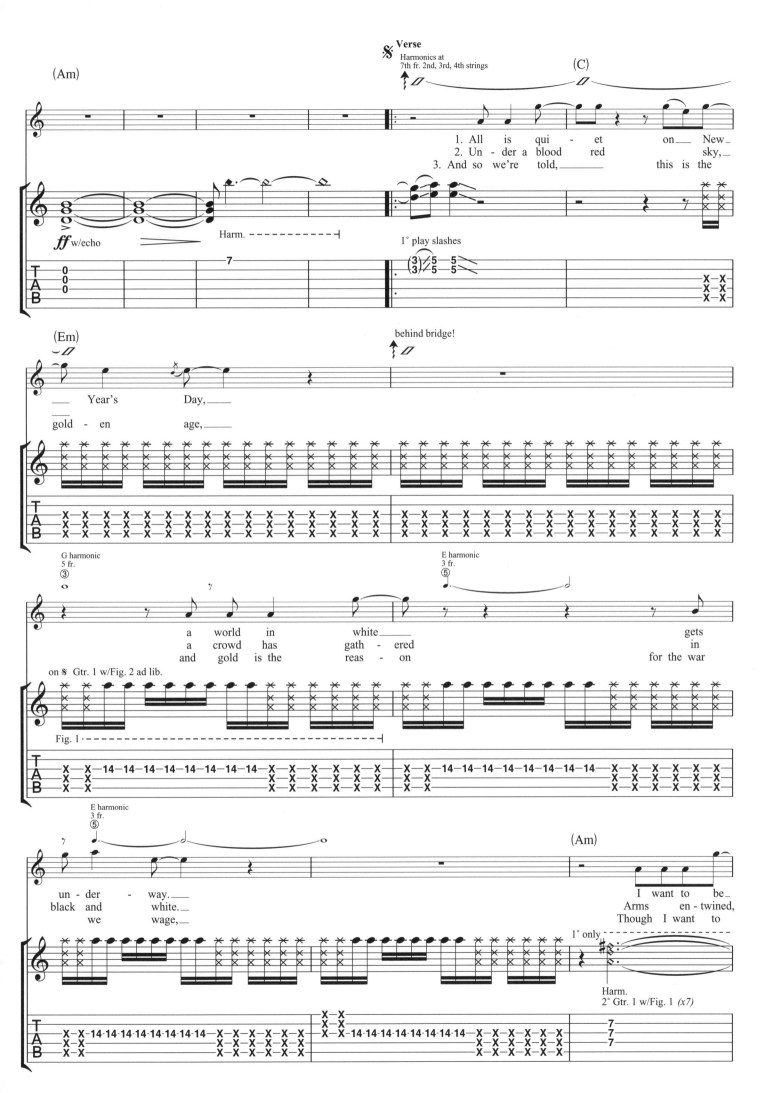

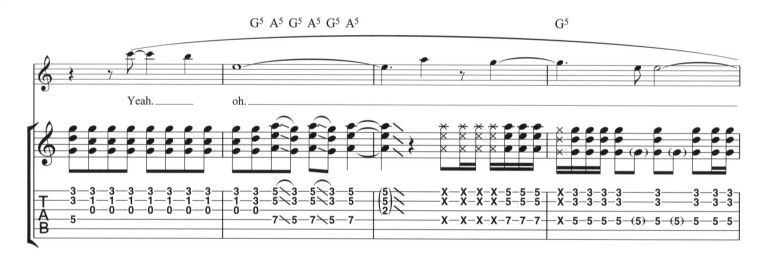

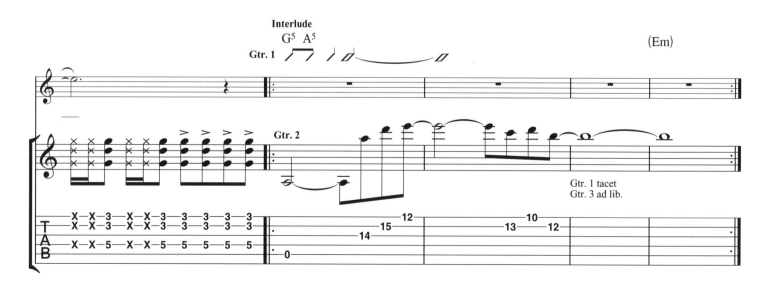

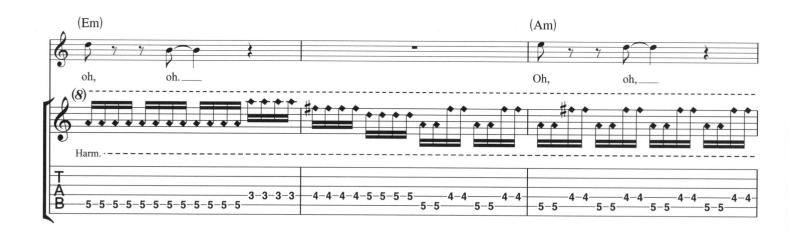

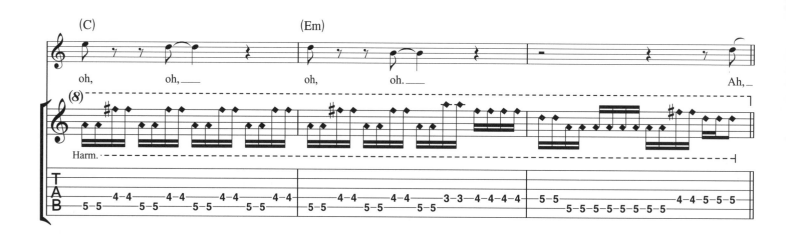

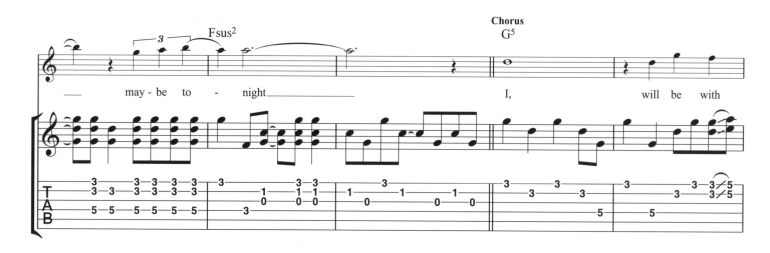

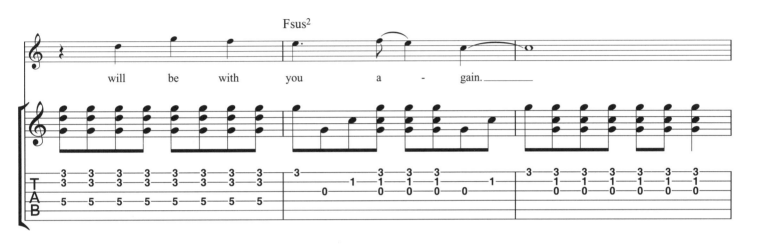

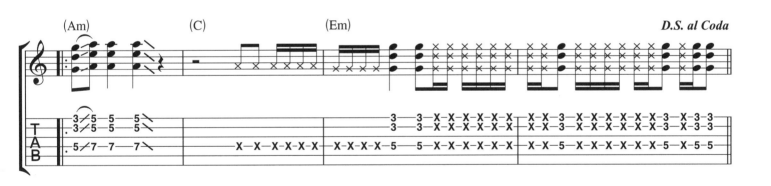

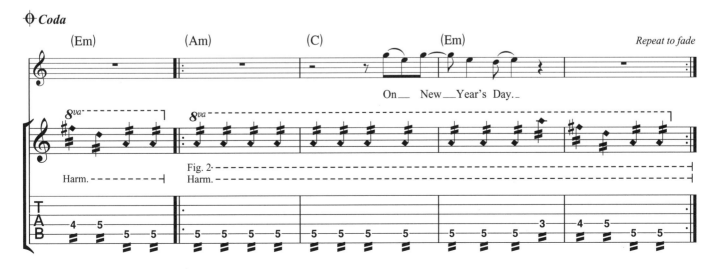

Two Hearts Beat As One

Words & Music by U2

* Percussive rhythm around chord shapes - *ad lib.*

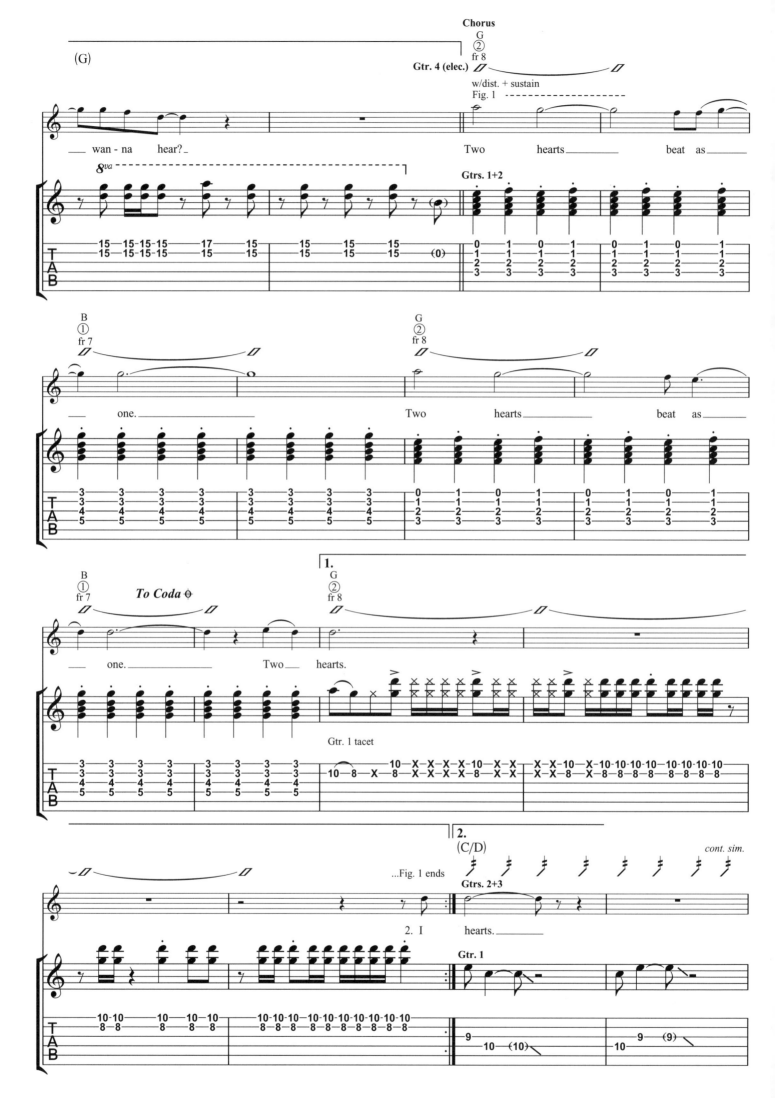

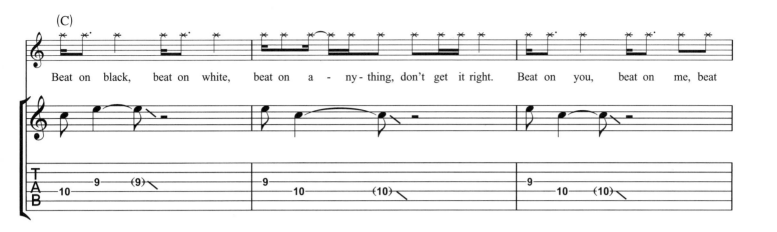

Beat on black, beat on white, beat on a - ny - thing, don't get it right. Beat on you, beat on me, beat

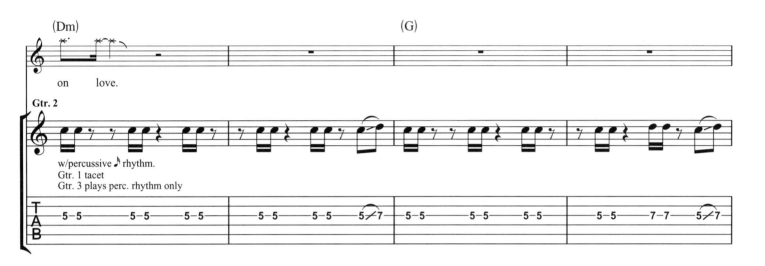

on love.

Gtr. 2

w/percussive ♪ rhythm.
Gtr. 1 tacet
Gtr. 3 plays perc. rhythm only

D.S. al Coda

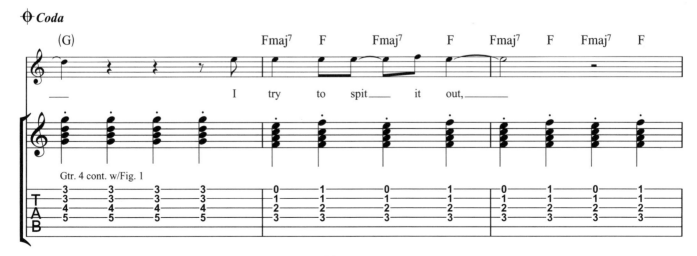

✠ *Coda*

I   try   to   spit___   it   out,___

Gtr. 4 cont. w/Fig. 1

Guitar Tablature Explained

Guitar music can be notated in three different ways: on a musical stave, in tablature, and in rhythm slashes.

RHYTHM SLASHES are written above the stave. Strum chords in the rhythm indicated. Round noteheads indicate single notes.

THE MUSICAL STAVE shows pitches and rhythms and is divided by lines into bars. Pitches are named after the first seven letters of the alphabet.

TABLATURE graphically represents the guitar fingerboard. Each horizontal line represents a string, and each number represents a fret.

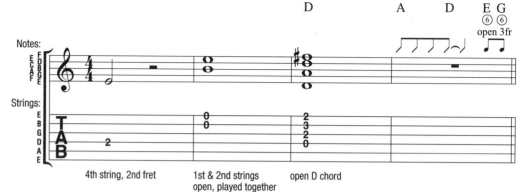

4th string, 2nd fret   1st & 2nd strings open, played together   open D chord

Definitions For Special Guitar Notation

SEMI-TONE BEND: Strike the note and bend up a semi-tone (1/2 step).

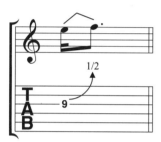

BEND & RELEASE: Strike the note and bend up as indicated, then release back to the original note.

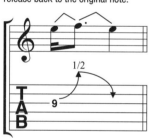

UNISON BEND: Strike the two notes simultaneously and bend the lower note up to the pitch of the higher.

VIBRATO: The string is vibrated by rapidly bending and releasing the note with the fretting hand.

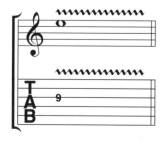

WHOLE-TONE BEND: Strike the note and bend up a whole-tone (whole step).

COMPOUND BEND & RELEASE: Strike the note and bend up and down in the rhythm indicated.

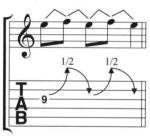

BEND & RESTRIKE: Strike the note and bend as indicated then restrike the string where the symbol occurs.

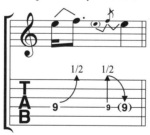

HAMMER-ON: Strike the first note with one finger, then sound the second note (on the same string) with another finger by fretting it without picking.

GRACE NOTE BEND: Strike the note and bend as indicated. Play the first note as quickly as possible.

PRE-BEND: Bend the note as indicated, then strike it.

BEND, HOLD AND RELEASE: Same as bend and release but hold the bend for the duration of the tie.

PULL-OFF: Place both fingers on the notes to be sounded, strike the first note and without picking, pull the finger off to sound the second note.

QUARTER-TONE BEND: Strike the note and bend up a 1/4 step.

PRE-BEND & RELEASE: Bend the note as indicated. Strike it and release the note back to the original pitch.

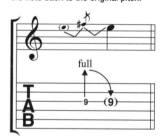

BEND AND TAP: Bend the note as indicated and tap the higher fret while still holding the bend.

LEGATO SLIDE (GLISS): Strike the first note and then slide the same fret-hand finger up or down to the second note. The second note is not struck.

NOTE: The speed of any bend is indicated by the music notation and tempo.

SHIFT SLIDE (GLISS & RESTRIKE): Same as legato slide, except the second note is struck.

TRILL: Very rapidly alternate between the notes indicated by continuously hammering on and pulling off.

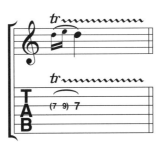

TAPPING: Hammer ("tap") the fret indicated with the pick-hand index or middle finger and pull off to the note fretted by the fret hand.

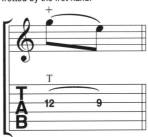

PICK SCRAPE: The edge of the pick is rubbed down (or up) the string, producing a scratchy sound.

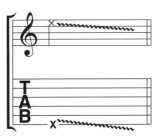

MUFFLED STRINGS: A percussive sound is produced by laying the fret hand across the string(s) without depressing, and striking them with the pick hand.

NATURAL HARMONIC: Strike the note while the fret-hand lightly touches the string directly over the fret indicated.

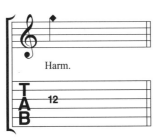

PINCH HARMONIC: The note is fretted normally and a harmonic is produced by adding the edge of the thumb or the tip of the index finger of the pick hand to the normal pick attack.

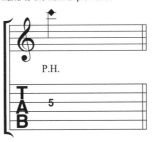

HARP HARMONIC: The note is fretted normally and a harmonic is produced by gently resting the pick hand's index finger directly above the indicated fret (in brackets) while plucking the appropriate string.

PALM MUTING: The note is partially muted by the pick hand lightly touching the string(s) just before the bridge.

RAKE: Drag the pick across the strings indicated with a single motion.

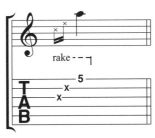

TREMOLO PICKING: The note is picked as rapidly and continuously as possible.

ARPEGGIATE: Play the notes of the chord indicated by quickly rolling them from bottom to top.

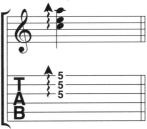

SWEEP PICKING: Rhythmic downstroke and/or upstroke motion across the strings.

VIBRATO DIVE BAR AND RETURN: The pitch of the note or chord is dropped a specific number of steps (in rhythm) then returned to the original pitch.

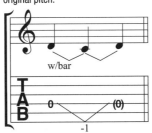

VIBRATO BAR SCOOP: Depress the bar just before striking the note, then quickly release the bar.

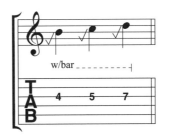

VIBRATO BAR DIP: Strike the note and then immediately drop a specific number of steps, then release back to the original pitch.

additional musical definitions

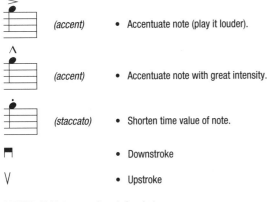

(accent) • Accentuate note (play it louder).

(accent) • Accentuate note with great intensity.

(staccato) • Shorten time value of note.

• Downstroke

V • Upstroke

NOTE: Tablature numbers in brackets mean:
1. The note is sustained, but a new articulation (such as hammer on or slide) begins.
2. A note may be fretted but not necessarily played.

D.%. al Coda

D.C. al Fine

tacet

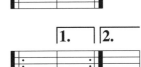

1. | 2.

• Go back to the sign (%), then play until the bar marked *To Coda* ⊕ then skip to the section marked ⊕ *Coda*.

• Go back to the beginning of the song and play until the bar marked *Fine*.

• Instrument is silent (drops out).

• Repeat bars between signs.

• When a repeated section has different endings, play the first ending only the first time and the second ending only the second time.

CD Track Listing

Full instrumental performances (with guitar)...

1 Out Of Control
2 I Will Follow
3 The Electric Co.
4 Gloria
5 Sunday Bloody Sunday
6 New Year's Day
7 Two Hearts Beat As One

Backing tracks only (without guitar)...

8 Out Of Control
9 I Will Follow
10 The Electric Co.
11 Gloria
12 Sunday Bloody Sunday
13 New Year's Day
14 Two Hearts Beat As One

All tracks:
(U2) Blue Mountain Music Limited.

To remove your CD from the plastic sleeve, lift the
small lip on the side to break the perforated strip.
Replace the disc after use for convenient storage.